REASONS TO CARE ABOUT
ELEPHANTS

[Animals in Peril]

Mary Firestone

Enslow Publishers, Inc.

40 Industrial Road
Box 398
Berkeley Heights, NJ 07922
USA
http://www.enslow.com

Library of Congress Cataloguing-in-Publication Data
Firestone, Mary.
  Top 50 reasons to care about elephants : animals in peril / by Mary Firestone.
    p. cm. – (Top 50 reasons to care about endangered animals)
  Includes bibliographical references and index.
  Summary: "Readers will learn about an elephant's ears, trunk and teeth, what they eat, their ancestors, the different kinds of elephants, and why they are on the endangered animals list"–Provided by publisher.
  ISBN 978-0-7660-3454-9
  1. Elephants–Juvenile literature. 2. Endangered species–Juvenile literature. I. Title. II. Title: Top fifty reasons to care about elephants.
  QL737.P98F57 2010
  599.67–dc22

                            2008048690

Printed in the United States of America

092009 Lake Book Manufacturing, Inc., Melrose Park, IL

10 9 8 7 6 5 4 3 2 1

To Our Readers: We have done our best to make sure all Internet Addresses in this book were active and appropriate when we went to press. However, the author and the publisher have no control over and assume no liability for the material available on those Internet sites or on other Web sites they may link to. Any comments or suggestions can be sent by e-mail to comments@enslow.com or to the address on the back cover.

Photographs: Jan Rysavy/iStockphoto, cover inset, 1; Mitsuaki Iwago/Minden Pictures, 1; Karl Ammann/Nature Picture Library, 4; Red Line Editorial, 6; Patricio Robles Gil/Nature Picture Library, 8; Peter Malsbur /iStockphoto, 9; Pete Oxford/Nature Picture Library, 11, 51; Neil Wigmore/iStockphoto, 12; AP Images/Nick Ut, 15; Dorling Kindersley/DK Images, 16; Karl Ammann/Nature Picture Library, 18, 48; Cat London/iStockphoto, 20; Peter Blackwell/Nature Picture Library, 21, 40; Anup Shah/Nature Picture Library, 22, 29, 45, 71, 82; Cay-Uwe Kulzer/iStockphoto, 23; Nick Garbutt/Nature Picture Library, 25; iStockphoto, 26, 67; Hedda Gjerpen/iStockphoto, 27; Paul Lang/iStockphoto, 28; Chris Fertnig/iStockphoto, 30; Duncan Noakes/iStockphoto, 31; Achim Prill/iStockphoto, 32; Martina Berg/iStockphoto, 34; Dave Johnston/iStockphoto, 35; Suresh Menon/iStockphoto, 36 (top); Bruce Block/iStockphoto, 36 (bottom); Richard du Toit/Nature Picture Library, 39, 88; Denis Ananiadis/iStockphoto, 41; Lorenzo Pastore/iStockphoto, 42; Henk Bentlage/iStockphoto, 44; Tony Heald/Nature Picture Library, 47, 52, 53; Nico Smit/iStockphoto, 49; Ewen Cameron/iStockphoto, 50; Mark Rigby/iStockphoto, 54; Paul Bamforth/iStockphoto, 57; Sunil Kumar/iStockphoto, 58; AP Images, 61; John Hemmings/Shutterstock Images, 62; Photo Library, 65; Gregor Erdmann/iStockphoto, 66; Wendy Conway/iStockphoto, 68; Mark Atkins/iStockphoto, 72; Bruce Davidson/Nature Picture Library, 75; Ian Redmond/Nature Picture Library, 76; Vivek Menon/Nature Picture Library, 79; Luciano Adriani/AP Images, 80; Michael Sheehan/iStockphoto, 85; Toby Sinclair/Nature Picture Library, 86; Hansjoerg Richter/iStockphoto, 89; Simon King/Nature Picture Library, 91; Sarah Byatt/Nature Picture Library, 92; Frank Parker/iStockphoto, 94; Zenz Sonnema/iStockphoto, 95; Marcel Pelletier/iStockphoto, 96; Heiko Potthoff/iStockphoto, 97; Andrea Hill/iStockphoto, 99

Cover caption: An African elephant calf stands with its mother.
Mitsuaki Iwago/Minden Pictures

CONTENTS

ENDANGERED ELEPHANTS

Elephants are unique animals found in Africa and Asia. They are well known for their enormous size, wide ears, and long trunks. Elephants are intelligent and caring. But elephants are at risk of extinction.

Poaching and loss of habitat are the most important threats to the elephant's way of life. In the 1970s and 1980s, poaching cut the African elephant population in half. Despite harsh laws against poaching, elephants continue to be hunted for their ivory tusks.

These large animals need lots of land. Elephants travel long distances. They eat grasses and clear spaces that allow their habitat to thrive. Their habitat is shrinking. Soon, the land may not be able to support the elephants and the other animals that live there. Elephants are already turning to farmland and populated areas in search for food.

The only way for elephants to survive is through human action. We need to correct the actions that are hurting elephants. We can protect elephant habitats. We can support laws against poaching. If we are aware of how our actions affect other animals and their habitats, in time, elephants may thrive again.

◀ ELEPHANTS ARE ENDANGERED.

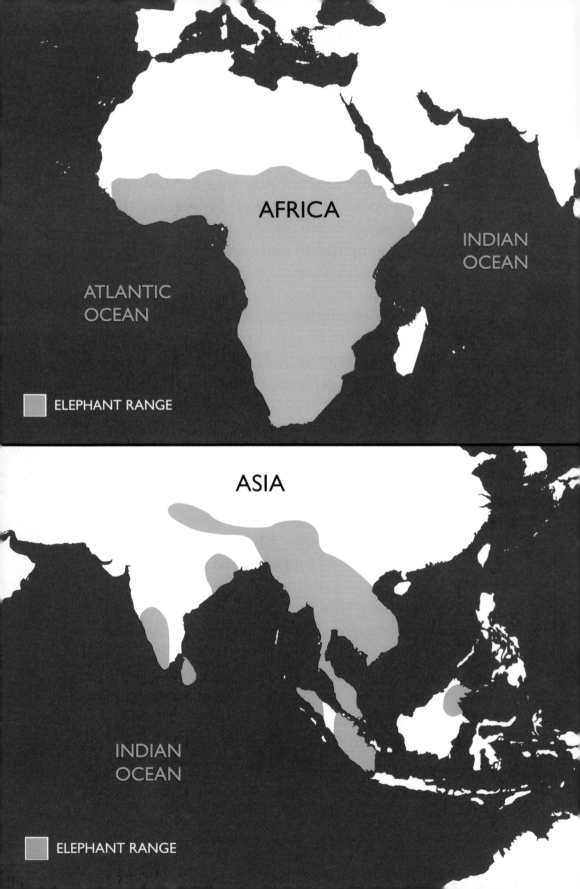

AFRICA

INDIAN
OCEAN

ATLANTIC
OCEAN

ELEPHANT RANGE

ASIA

INDIAN
OCEAN

ELEPHANT RANGE

Elephants Have Been Here for Millions of Years

In the predawn darkness of southern Africa, a herd of wild elephants is rising from their sleep. For such massive animals, they make surprisingly little noise as they walk. They will spend the day traveling the same routes as their ancestors as they forage for food, bathe in waterholes and rivers, and rest in the shade of the forest. This routine has been the way of elephants for millions of years. And yet, it might end forever if we are not careful.

◄ TOP: ELEPHANTS LIVE IN THE FORESTS AND SAVANNAS OF AFRICA. BOTTOM: ELEPHANTS LIVE IN SOUTHEAST ASIA.

There Are Two Kinds of African Elephants

Two species of elephants in Africa are generally recognized by scientists today: the savanna elephant and the forest elephant. Savanna elephants get their name from their habitat. A savanna is land with grasslands, short trees, and shrubs scattered widely throughout open spaces.

▼ AFRICAN FOREST ELEPHANT

▲ AFRICAN SAVANNA ELEPHANT

The savanna elephant is the largest living land animal. Its tusks curve and point outward. Savanna elephants live on the grassy plains and woodlands south of the Sahara Desert, in eastern and southern Africa.

The forest elephant is smaller than the savanna elephant and has darker skin. Its long tusks point downward. Forest elephants live in central and western Africa. They are more threatened than the savanna elephants because of poaching and habitat loss.

[The savanna elephant's scientific name is *Loxodonta africana.* Forest elephants are *Loxodonta cyclotis.*]

There Are Four Kinds of Asian Elephants

Asian elephants are smaller than African savanna elephants. Asian elephants live in the forests and jungles of Cambodia, China, India, Indonesia, Malaysia, Myanmar, Sri Lanka, Thailand, and Vietnam. Four types of elephants now live in Asia and India: the Indian, the Sumatran, the Sri Lankan, and the Bornean.

Asian communities have densely populated areas that are beginning to take over elephant habitats. This has been the biggest problem facing Asian elephants. Loss of habitat for elephants means loss of food, because they must forage over large areas to meet their daily needs for vegetation.

[All Asian elephants share the same first two words of their scientific name. The scientific name of the Asian elephant is *Elephas maximas.*]

▶ INDIAN ELEPHANTS ARE ONE OF THE FOUR TYPES OF ASIAN ELEPHANTS.

REASON TO CARE # 4

Elephants Are the Largest Land Animals

Male savanna elephants in Africa are the largest land animals living today. Male savanna elephants stand from 10 to 13 feet (3 to 4 meters) tall and can weigh as much as 15,400 pounds (7,000 kilograms). African elephant females are about 9 feet (2.8 meters) tall and weigh around 8,000 pounds (3,600 kilograms).

The largest Asian elephant is the Indian male. It can stand 8 to 10 feet (2.5 to 3 meters) tall at the shoulder and weighs up to 10,000 pounds (4,500 kilograms). Indian female elephants are about 8 feet (2.5 meters) tall and weigh around 6,600 pounds (3,000 kilograms).

[A prehistoric dwarf elephant once lived on islands in the Mediterranean Sea. These elephants were only 3 feet (1 meter) tall.]

◄ THIS ELEPHANT IS MUCH BIGGER THAN A CAR.

Elephants Lived Around the World

Elephants are part of an order of animals known as Proboscidea. Millions of years ago, 350 different species of elephants roamed Earth's continents. Elephant fossils have been found on all continents except Australia and Antarctica. Today, elephant populations are found only in Africa and Asia.

The earliest proboscideans lived around 50 million years ago. They didn't look much like today's elephants. They were only about 3 feet (1 meter) tall, which is the size of a pig. They had no trunk whatsoever.

[Ancient mammoths and mastodons were related, but they were not the same species. Mastodons were smaller than mammoths and had straighter tusks. Mammoths had ridged molars for eating grass, while mastodons had cone-shaped teeth for eating trees and shrubs.]

▶ A SCIENTIST EXPOSES THE REMAINS OF A PREHISTORIC MAMMOTH.

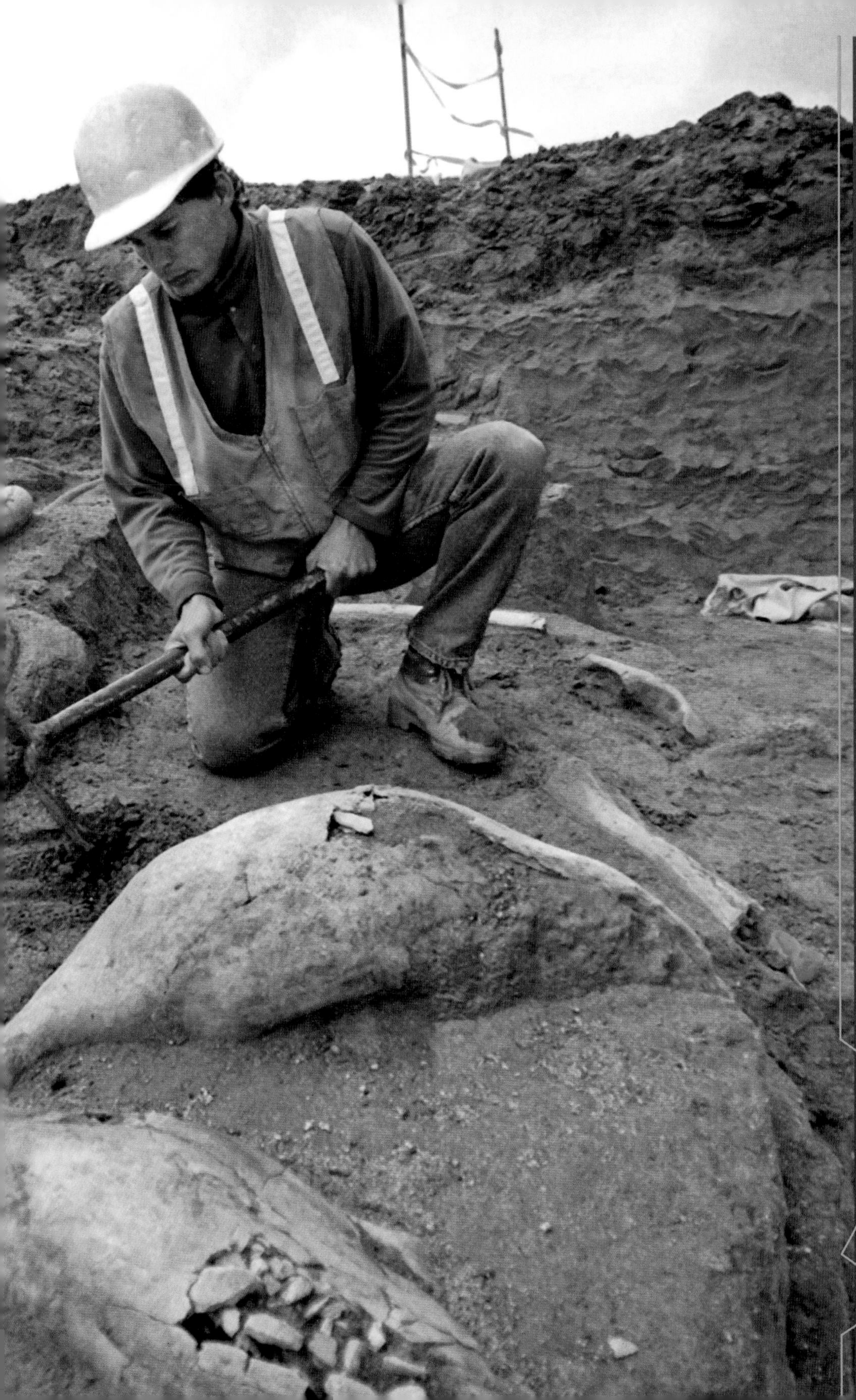

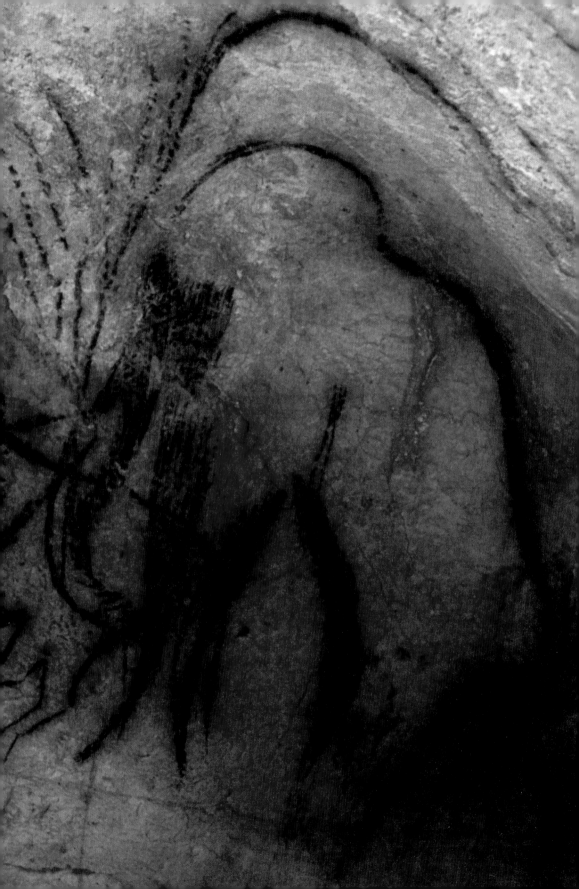

REASON TO CARE # 6

The Woolly Mammoth Was the Elephant's Relative

The woolly mammoth was a prehistoric relative of the elephant. It adapted to live in cold climates, with a woolly coat of hair 3 feet long. Standing 14 feet (4.3 meters) tall with curved tusks 16 feet long, it must have been a formidable sight to prehistoric people.

But this did not stop hunters from killing woolly mammoths for food and hides. Ancient people even created sculptures of mammoths from ivory and painted mammoths on cave walls. Most woolly mammoths became extinct 10,000 years ago, but one group off the northeast coast of Siberia lived until 3,800 years ago.

[In 2007, archaeologists found the oldest carving of a woolly mammoth known to modern science at the Vogelherd Cave in Germany. At 35,000 years old, the newly found Ice Age figure is still in excellent condition. Unlike the mammoth, it is tiny. At 2.2 inches long, the carving weighs .26 ounces.]

◄ THIS ANCIENT CAVE PAINTING SHOWS A MAMMOTH.

ELEPHANT BIOLOGY

REASON TO CARE # 7

Elephants Live Longer than Other Mammals

A baby elephant, or calf, grows inside its mother's body for twenty-two months. Newborn elephants weigh approximately 250 pounds (110 kilograms) and stand 3 feet (1 meter) tall at birth. Within fifteen minutes of being born, baby elephants can stand up. Within one hour, they are on the move with the herd.

For its first year of life, a calf remains very close to its mother. It feeds on her milk for two full years. The youngster learns from its mother how to drink water and use its trunk to grip grasses. It depends on its mother until it is about ten years old. At around age thirteen, elephants are old enough to mate.

Elephants in the wild live to be sixty or seventy years old if they are not killed by poachers, drought, or disease. Some elephants in captivity live even longer. They live longer than any other land mammals except humans.

◀ ELEPHANTS DEPEND ON THEIR MOTHERS UNTIL THEY ARE TEN YEARS OLD.

Elephants Eat a Lot of Food

It takes a lot of food to feed an animal as large as an elephant. Adult elephants eat about 300 pounds of food each day and drink as much as 40 gallons of water. Elephants can go a long time without water, even as long as three days. This is a good ability, as dry seasons often include periods of drought.

▼ ELEPHANTS EAT MANY DIFFERENT TYPES OF VEGETATION.

▲ ELEPHANTS CAN USE THEIR TUSKS TO DIG FOR SALT AND MINERALS.

Elephants are herbivores and their diet mainly includes grass. They also eat leaves, bark, fruit, twigs, water plants, and seeds, depending on their habitats.

To get fruit from trees, elephants wrap their trunks around the tree to shake the fruit from the branches. They may eat figs, coffee berries, and mangoes. In dry seasons, elephants eat bark, using their tusks to strip it from the tree.

Another thing elephants must have is salt. Salt can be found in the ground, and elephants use their tusks like shovels to dig salt from the soil and rocks. They also eat bits of soil, which contain important minerals.

Elephant Tusks Are Great Tools

An elephant's tusks are incisor teeth, and they grow continuously throughout its lifetime. The heaviest tusks known today weigh 225 and 236 pounds each, and came from Mount Kilimanjaro. The longest existing tusks are 10.99 and 11.45 feet each, and came from eastern Congo. Male and female African elephants both have tusks.

▼ SOMETIMES ELEPHANTS REST THEIR TRUNKS ON THEIR TUSKS.

▲ YOU CAN TELL THIS ELEPHANT IS "RIGHT-TUSKED" BECAUSE THE RIGHT TUSK IS SHORTER THAN THE LEFT.

Similar to right- and left-handed humans, elephants are right- or left-tusked. This means they use one tusk more often, leaving it worn and shortened.

Asian male elephants also have tusks, but many males are tuskless. Asian female tusks are small and sometimes completely hidden, or sometimes they do not have tusks at all.

Baby elephants are born with milk tusks, similar to human baby teeth. These fall out when they get older, at around six to twelve months.

Tusks are great tools. Elephants use them to dig for plant roots, water, and salt. They can also be a good resting place for weary trunks. Tusks can lift loads of up to 2,000 pounds.

An Elephant Has Very Large Teeth

Besides their tusks, elephants have only four molar teeth. These teeth are replaced as they are worn away, up to six times throughout an elephant's life. Front molars wear down and drop out, and the back molars gradually push forward to replace them. Elephant teeth are like everything else about elephants: very large. An elephant molar weighs around 9 pounds and is 1 foot long.

When an elephant's final set of molars wears down, it cannot chew its food anymore. An elephant does not die from old age but from malnutrition.

▶ AN ELEPHANT'S BACK TEETH, OR MOLARS, ARE VERY LARGE.

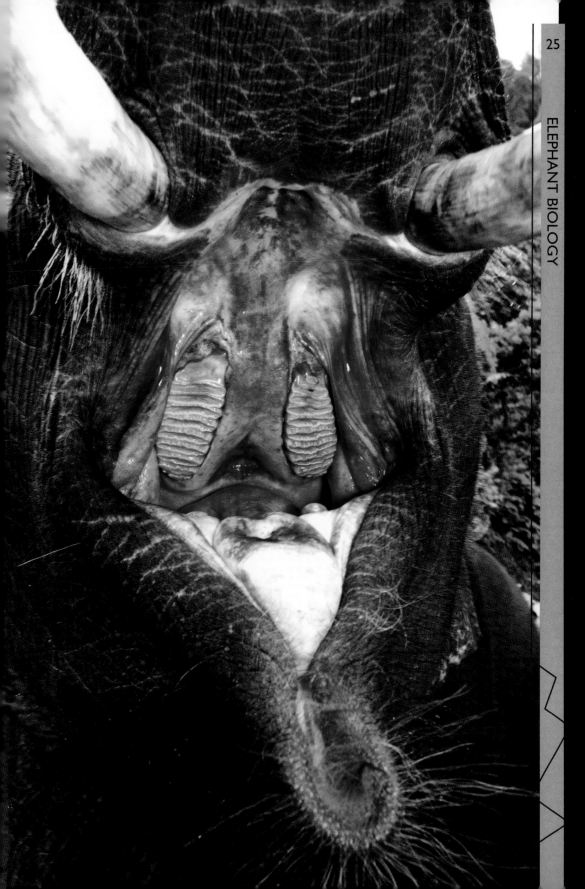

Elephants Use Their Ears to Stay Cool

African elephants have large heads, with a smooth curve on their foreheads. Asian elephants also have large heads, but their foreheads have two wide bumps.

Elephant ears are shaped like triangles. African elephants' ears are very large, cover their shoulders, and resemble the shape of Africa.

▼ AFRICAN ELEPHANTS HAVE LARGE EARS.

▲ ASIAN ELEPHANT EARS ARE SMALLER THAN AFRICAN ELEPHANT EARS.

Asian elephants' ears are small by comparison and barely touch their shoulders. Their ears are said to be in the shape of India. Elephants flap their ears like fans to stay cool and to keep away insects.

Elephant Skin
Is Very Thick

Elephants have thick, wrinkled, gray skin, which hangs loosely in folds. Elephant skin is very heavy. It is about 1 inch thick and weighs about 2,000 pounds. But even though elephant skin is thick, it is also surprisingly tender. Insects, such as flies and mosquitoes, are able to bite into elephant flesh.

▼ ELEPHANT SKIN IS THICK AND WRINKLY.

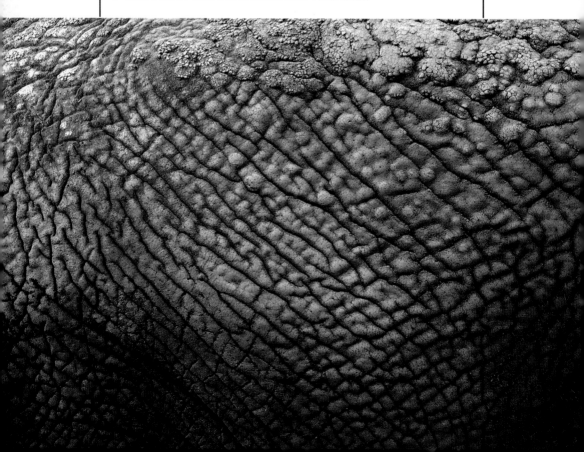

▲ ELEPHANTS SPLASH THEMSELVES TO KEEP COOL.

Elephants do not have sweat glands to help them stay cool. Instead, they stay cool by spraying water on themselves and wallowing in mud. Mud soothes their skin and protects it from the sun. Elephants also powder themselves with dust and take baths every day when enough water is available.

African elephants have dark gray skin, and their trunks have deep wrinkles. Most Asian elephants have light gray skin, and sometimes they even have white or pink areas. Asian elephant trunks have fewer wrinkles than the African elephant.

[Baby elephants have a light crop of black, brown, or reddish-brown hair, which disappears as the calf grows older. Adult elephants are almost hairless, except for the tips of their tails.]

Elephant Trunks Can Hold Water

An elephant's trunk is both a nose and an upper lip. An adult male trunk is around 5 feet long. Elephants use their trunks for breathing, bathing, smelling, and drinking water. To drink, elephants suck water up into their trunks and squirt it into their mouths. An adult elephant can hold as much as 3 gallons of water in its trunk.

▼ ELEPHANTS USE THEIR TRUNKS TO PUT FOOD INTO THEIR MOUTHS.

▲ ELEPHANTS DRINK BY SUCKING WATER INTO THEIR TRUNKS, THEN SQUIRTING IT INTO THEIR MOUTHS.

Elephants use their trunks to grip, throw, and lift things. The trunks are extremely strong. Elephants can use their trunks to carry heavy logs, but also to pick up small berries. When eating, elephants wind their trunks around branches, leaves, and grasses to pull the food into their mouths. Elephants greet each other by putting the tips of their trunks in each other's mouths. Baby elephants receive comfort from their mothers, who stroke them with their trunks. Young male elephants use their trunks to wrestle during play fights.

REASON TO CARE # 14

Elephants Have a Good Sense of Smell

Elephants depend on their sense of smell more than the rest of their senses. They wave their trunks in the air to smell food or to sense the presence of enemies. They can smell odors from more than 1 mile away.

Elephants' large ears help their sense of hearing. They also can hear and create sounds that humans cannot. They do this in a low vibration range called infrasound, which travels further than higher sound frequencies. This enables elephants to communicate with each other from distances of 2.5 miles or more.

An elephant's trunk is very sensitive. With the end of its trunk, an elephant can sense an object's shape, texture, and temperature.

Elephants have small eyes and they have difficulty turning their heads around. This limits their ability to see, so eyesight is not one of their strengths.

[Elephants have a good sense of balance. They can walk down steep, mountainous paths without losing their footing. In these situations, riders are safer on elephants than they are on horses.]

◀ ELEPHANTS HAVE SENSITIVE HEARING AND A STRONG SENSE OF SMELL.

Elephant Feet Change Size

When an elephant walks, its feet get bigger with each step and get smaller when lifted. If an elephant sinks into mud, it can free itself because its feet will become smaller. Elephant feet are round, and each foot has thick padding that cushions them as they walk.

Not all elephants have the same number of toes. African savanna elephants have four toes on their front feet and three on their back feet. Asian elephants and African forest elephants, however, have five toes on their front feet and four on their back feet.

▼ ASIAN ELEPHANTS HAVE MORE TOES THAN AFRICAN SAVANNA ELEPHANTS.

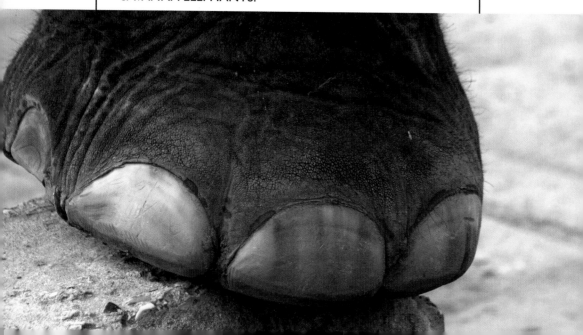

▲ ELEPHANTS ENJOY SWIMMING.

REASON TO CARE # 16

Elephants Are Great Swimmers

The elephant's normal walking speed is about 4 miles per hour. It can run in bursts of around 25 miles per hour when chasing predators away.

Elephants are excellent swimmers. They are able to stay in the water for six hours at a time without touching the bottom. When an elephant swims underwater, it raises its trunk above the surface, using it as a snorkel. Elephants can swim at 2 miles per hour.

ELEPHANT BEHAVIOR

REASON TO CARE # 17

Elephants Need Lots of Space

Elephants move as family units and groups in areas called ranges. The ranges provide all of the food, shelter, and water they need to survive.

For a species to survive, its habitat must provide enough space, food, and water. Elephants are herbivores and they eat enormous amounts of plants on a daily basis. Their habitat must include large land areas, or they can starve from the lack of vegetation. The savanna elephant thrives in a habitat of grasslands found in eastern and southern Africa, where there are plenty of edible bushes and shrubs.

Asian elephants and African forest elephants live mainly in woodland areas where they can feed on fruits, leaves, and branches. With tender grasses, warm marshy areas are another elephant habitat.

◀ TOP: ASIAN ELEPHANTS PREFER WOODLAND AREAS.
BOTTOM: SAVANNA ELEPHANTS ROAM GRASSLANDS.

Elephants Help Their Habitats Grow

According to scientists, a keystone species is an animal that transforms a habitat. Elephants transform habitats in so many ways that scientists have dubbed them a super keystone species.

What does it mean to transform a habitat? Elephants dig up dry riverbeds to find water, which provides water for other thirsty animals. When a hungry herd of elephants feasts on trees, shrubs, and bushes, they pull down branches and strip the bark clean. This is an act of pruning, which makes plants and trees grow back even stronger and thicker. Over time, this thicker growth provides more food than there had been before.

► ELEPHANT ACTIONS CAN TAKE DOWN TREES AND SHAPE THE ENVIRONMENT.

Elephants Help Smaller Animals

Elephants knock down trees to reach leaves and fruit. As the trees fall, shady areas in the forest get more sunlight. Forest floors become grasslands, providing new homes for animals and plants.

Elephants often do not eat all of the fruit on the fallen branches. This helps smaller animals that cannot reach high branches to find food. Traveling elephants also knock insects off plants. Small animals can eat these insects off the ground.

▼ AS ELEPHANTS EAT, FOOD DROPS TO THE GROUND AND FEEDS SMALLER ANIMALS.

▲ A DUNG BEETLE ROLLS DUNG INTO A BALL.

REASON TO CARE # 20

Elephant Dung Spreads Seeds

An elephant drops about 200 pounds of dung each day. An elephant's diet includes seeds. These seeds land on the ground still embedded in dung, ready to grow.

A type of beetle called the dung beetle thrives because of elephant dung. Females roll dung balls and lay a single egg in each one. The ball is food for the baby insect.

REASON TO CARE # 21

Elephants Are Smart

As the old saying goes, "an elephant never forgets." Science has linked brain size to intelligence, and the elephant's 10-pound brain is the largest among land animals. The area of the brain that stores memory is the largest portion of the elephant's brain. It is so large that it bulges out on both sides of the elephant's head. Scientists agree that elephants can remember things for a very long time, such as locations of remote watering holes and feeding areas.

Elephants also show their intelligence through their problem solving. As an alert for elephant crop raids, farmers placed wooden bells around elephants' necks. But the elephants figured it out. They stuffed the bells with grass to prevent them from ringing. This made it easy for them to sneak into farmers' fields at night to steal bananas.

◄ AN ELEPHANT'S INTELLIGENCE ALLOWS IT TO REMEMBER THE LOCATION OF FOOD SOURCES.

Elephant Trunks Are Like Human Hands

The elephant's soaring trumpet and the lion's roar are familiar sounds of the jungle. For elephants, this trumpeting blast means alarm or danger. Elephants have poor eyesight, so they must rely on these blasts of noise and other forms of communication to warn their herd and neighbors.

▼ IN MANY WAYS, ELEPHANTS USE THEIR TRUNKS LIKE HUMANS USE THEIR HANDS.

▲ ELEPHANTS CAN COMMUNICATE
BY TOUCHING TRUNKS.

Elephants also communicate through their sense of touch. Elephant trunks have a scattering of short hair at the tip and along the shaft, which increases its sensitivity to touch. In many ways, an elephant's trunk is similar to a human hand. Elephants even shake other elephants' trunks when they encounter each other in the wild.

When they are preparing to mate, elephants wind their trunks together, similar to how people hold hands. Their sensitive trunks communicate information about the other elephant.

[Field scientist Caitlin O'Connell noticed an elephant turn its head and lift up one foot. Other elephants nearby did the same. The elephants were listening through their limbs, sensing the vibration of the earth for approaching friends or foes.]

Elephants Live in Families

Elephants have close family bonds, and they express their love and affection for each other openly. The leader of a family group is usually the oldest female. One group will sometimes join another. Scientists call these larger groupings kin or bond groups. They believe that the group members are all related to one another. Large herds of elephants are made up of several kin groups and travel as one extra-large family.

Usually, herds range from six to twelve elephants, including an extended family of females and their male offspring. Sometimes the larger groups split up and travel separately, but they later rejoin the larger group. Males usually leave the group when they reach their teens. Males usually travel alone, or sometimes form temporary, unstable herds.

[A population consists of all the elephants that share an area. It includes the females and all related kin, the males traveling alone, and the male herds. Populations vary from a few hundred elephants to several thousand.]

▶ ELEPHANTS ARE SOCIAL AND LIVE IN HERDS.

REASON TO CARE # 24

Matriarchs Lead Elephant Families

The leader of the family is the oldest female, called the matriarch. She has a lifetime of experience. She knows the locations of watering holes and feeding areas. She makes decisions about how fast and how long the herd will travel.

The matriarch's herd is made up of her adult daughters and sisters and their children. Young male elephants remain near their mothers until they are adults.

▼ THE MATRIARCH WATCHES OUT FOR HER HERD.

▲ BULL ELEPHANTS ONLY JOIN FEMALE HERDS TO MATE.

REASON TO CARE # 25

Bulls Travel
Alone

Adult male elephants are called bulls. They are larger than females and do not live with the matriarch's herd. Bulls often travel alone, but sometimes they travel in herds. However, these herds are usually not relatives. They travel together for only a few weeks or sometimes only a few days. Males only join female herds when a female is ready to mate. Even then, he stays only for a few days.

Families Protect Baby Elephants

A mother elephant gives birth standing up. Other females surround her to protect her and her infant. Once born, the calf is covered in a birth membrane. The mother and her female relatives work together to pull off the membrane. Using their trunks, they gently urge the baby to stand. Soon, the mother is pulling the infant toward her with her trunk to nurse.

▼ ALL OF THE FEMALES IN AN ELEPHANT FAMILY WATCH OUT FOR THE CALVES.

▲ ADULT ELEPHANTS HELP YOUNG CALVES KEEP UP.

Elephant mothers have a lot of help raising their youngsters. Baby elephants stand a better chance of surviving when other female elephants in the herd help out. Adolescent females practice nursing calves even though they are not producing milk. They protect calves and play with them. When a calf sounds distressed, all the females in the herd go to its rescue.

Elephants Care About Each Other

Mother elephants are very protective of their young. They will not hesitate to charge or even trample anything that threatens their safety. The matriarch of a herd will put herself at risk by standing up to poachers while her family runs to safety.

In recent years, elephants have attacked people and destroyed villages near their habitats. Researchers suggest that elephants are angry about habitat loss and killings by humans.

▼ ELEPHANTS MOURN THE DEATHS OF FAMILY MEMBERS.

▲ ELEPHANTS WILL CHARGE IF THEY FEEL THREATENED.

Orphaned calves that saw their mothers killed often wake up in the night screaming. Researchers say these baby elephants are suffering from post-traumatic stress disorder. Soldiers sometimes suffer from this disorder after being in a war.

When elephant family members or friends are ill or dying, elephants console and stay near them. When a family member dies, elephants cover the body with leaves and branches, resembling a burial. Elephants grieve the loss of their family members by standing nearby for days.

REASON TO CARE # 28

Elephants Protect Themselves from Enemies

Life for elephants can be challenging. In addition to the constant need to stay on the move to find adequate food and water, they must watch out for predators. An elephant's best protection is its tusks. If a lion charges an elephant, the elephant's tusks are strong enough to lift the lion and toss it to the ground. Seeing an angry, thundering elephant must be a terrifying sight. It is easy to see why elephants have very few predators!

Elephants also rely on their keen sense of hearing for protection. Their huge ears capture the slightest sound, keeping them aware of any danger. When a family member is sick or injured, elephant families form a circle around it to protect it from predators.

◄ THREATENED ELEPHANTS CAN ATTACK THEIR ENEMIES WITH THEIR DANGEROUS TUSKS.

Elephants
Have Routines

Jane Goodall, a naturalist famous for studying gorillas in their natural habitat, also observed elephants in Africa. She recorded their daily habits. She discovered that they have daily routines just as humans do.

On a typical day, the group she studied got up before sunrise to avoid moving in the midday heat. After a bit of grazing, the herd followed the matriarch to the watering hole where the elephants drank, sprayed water on themselves, and wallowed in the mud. By midmorning, the elephants stopped and rested in the shade. Adult elephants dozed while standing up, gently moving their ears to fan themselves. The elephants walked for 10 miles that day, stopping for the night around midnight. They all lay down for four hours of deep sleep, some of them breaking out with loud snores.

[Goodall found that elephants spend sixteen hours a day eating and foraging.]

▶ JANE GOODALL STUDIED THE DAILY ACTIVITIES OF ELEPHANTS, INCLUDING MUD-WALLOWING.

ELEPHANTS IN CULTURE

REASON TO CARE # 30

Asian Cultures Honor an Elephant God

The elephant is highly regarded in many Asian cultures. In India, the Hindu deity Ganesha is worshipped as a god of wisdom, good fortune, and remover of obstacles.

In statue form, Ganesha is shown with a human body and an elephant head. The human body represents his earthly existence. The elephant head represents his soul. It is a reminder of his wisdom and understanding.

◄ GANESHA IS THE HINDU GOD OF WISDOM AND GOOD FORTUNE.

Elephants Perform in Circuses

The first elephants came to the United States at the end of the eighteenth century. By the mid-nineteenth century, elephants were the stars of circuses that traveled the nation in wagons and railroad cars. Elephants drew curious crowds to see them perform. However, these early circus elephants were often chained and unable to move around. Trainers used painful methods to teach the elephants tricks.

Today, better regulations protect circus animals. Circuses employ veterinarians to look out for the animals' welfare. However, many animal rights groups believe that circus elephants still suffer during their training. These groups think that elephants should not perform in circuses. Some cities have banned live animals in circuses, and elephant performances remain controversial.

[The most famous circus elephant is Jumbo. Jumbo was the star of P.T. Barnum's "Greatest Show On Earth" until he died in 1885. His skeleton is kept at the American Museum of Natural History in New York.]

► CIRCUS ELEPHANTS HAVE TRAVELED THE COUNTRY IN TRAINS SINCE THE MID-NINETEENTH CENTURY.

REASON TO CARE # 32

Elephants
Are Artists

Elephants are intelligent and share many qualities we think of as human. They form close family bonds and can come up with complex solutions to problems. In captivity, some elephants even have a talent for painting. Elephant caretakers provide brushes, paper, and paint, and assist elephants in making artwork.

Many elephant paintings are "abstract"—a series of colorful brushstrokes or blotches made however the elephant wants. Some elephants are trained by humans to make a planned series of brushstrokes. With this training, they can create realistic elephants, flowers, and landscapes.

The Asian Elephant Art and Conservation Project sells artwork created by elephants. The paintings sell at prices ranging from a few hundred dollars to several thousand. The money is used for elephant care and to support mahouts. A mahout is a trainer who directs elephants that work in logging or pull other heavy loads for people. Many elephants and mahouts in Asia are unemployed because much of the forests have been cut down. Painting lets elephants and their mahouts make money.

◄ AN ELEPHANT PAINTS WITH GUIDANCE FROM ITS TRAINER.

Ancient Egyptians Valued Ivory

Ivory from elephant tusks has a long history of being valuable. Objects made from ivory were first created in large numbers around 4000 B.C., when Egyptians established ivory carving shops. There, workers carved statues and other objects from elephant and hippopotamus tusks. The ivory was worked in ways similar to wood and was carved into game pieces, spoons, combs, bracelets, knife handles, and writing tablets.

Around 2500 B.C., Egyptians decorated their caskets and furniture with ivory. The ancient Greeks created ivory and gold statues of gods and goddesses, such as Athena. Romans, too, used ivory to make combs, buttons, and hair ornaments.

[Although ivory was popular in the past, today it is illegal to buy and sell ivory.]

▶ THESE ANTIQUE CHINESE CHESS PIECES ARE MADE OF IVORY.

Elephants Are Valued Workers

Elephants have been caught and trained to do work for more than five thousand years. Elephants can move logs and other objects with their tusks and trunks.

The elephants of Sri Lanka, an island nation off the coast of India, have been an important part of that nation's traditions and religious activities for five thousand years. The kings of Sri Lanka captured and kept them in stables.

▼ MAHOUTS USE ELEPHANTS TO TRANSPORT HEAVY LOADS.

▲ ELEPHANTS CAN USE THEIR TRUNKS TO MOVE HEAVY OBJECTS, SUCH AS THESE LOGS.

In the fifth century B.C., the kings gave the elephant protection by law. The penalty for killing one was death.

In ancient times, elephants were used in war for transporting soldiers and weapons. Because of their size, elephants could ram barricades and swing chains with their trunks to prevent enemy contact.

Even today, Asian elephants work with mahouts, who drive elephants and teach them commands for use in logging. African elephants have also been trained to lift and pull heavy loads.

THREATS TO ELEPHANTS

REASON TO CARE # 35

All Elephants Are Threatened

The International Union for the Conservation of Nature and Natural Resources (IUCN) is the world's authority on the conservation status of species. They created the IUCN Red List of Threatened Species in 1963. This list includes the conservation status of both plant and animal species.

Conservationists consider all elephants to be threatened, which means they could become extinct. Some elephants are at greater risk than others. In some areas of Africa, elephant numbers are increasing. In Asia the numbers of elephants are decreasing.

In 1979, there were 1.3 million African elephants. Today, it is estimated that there are between 470,000 and 690,000 African elephants. There were around 100,000 Asian elephants in 1900, but today the population has recovered to between 38,000 and 51,000 animals.

◄ HUMAN ACTIONS THREATEN ELEPHANTS WITH EXTINCTION.

Climate Change Alters Elephant Habitats

Some scientists predict that climate change might have a big impact on the survival of elephants and other species. Dry lands in Africa may become even drier, with even less water and fewer plants.

In Sumatra, forests are destroyed to make room for palm oil plantations. This destroys the Asian elephant habitat while also contributing to climate change. Tropical forests are an important part of the earth's heating and cooling cycle because they help prevent carbon from reaching the atmosphere.

► CLIMATE CHANGE MIGHT MAKE IT HARDER FOR ELEPHANTS TO FIND FOOD AND WATER.

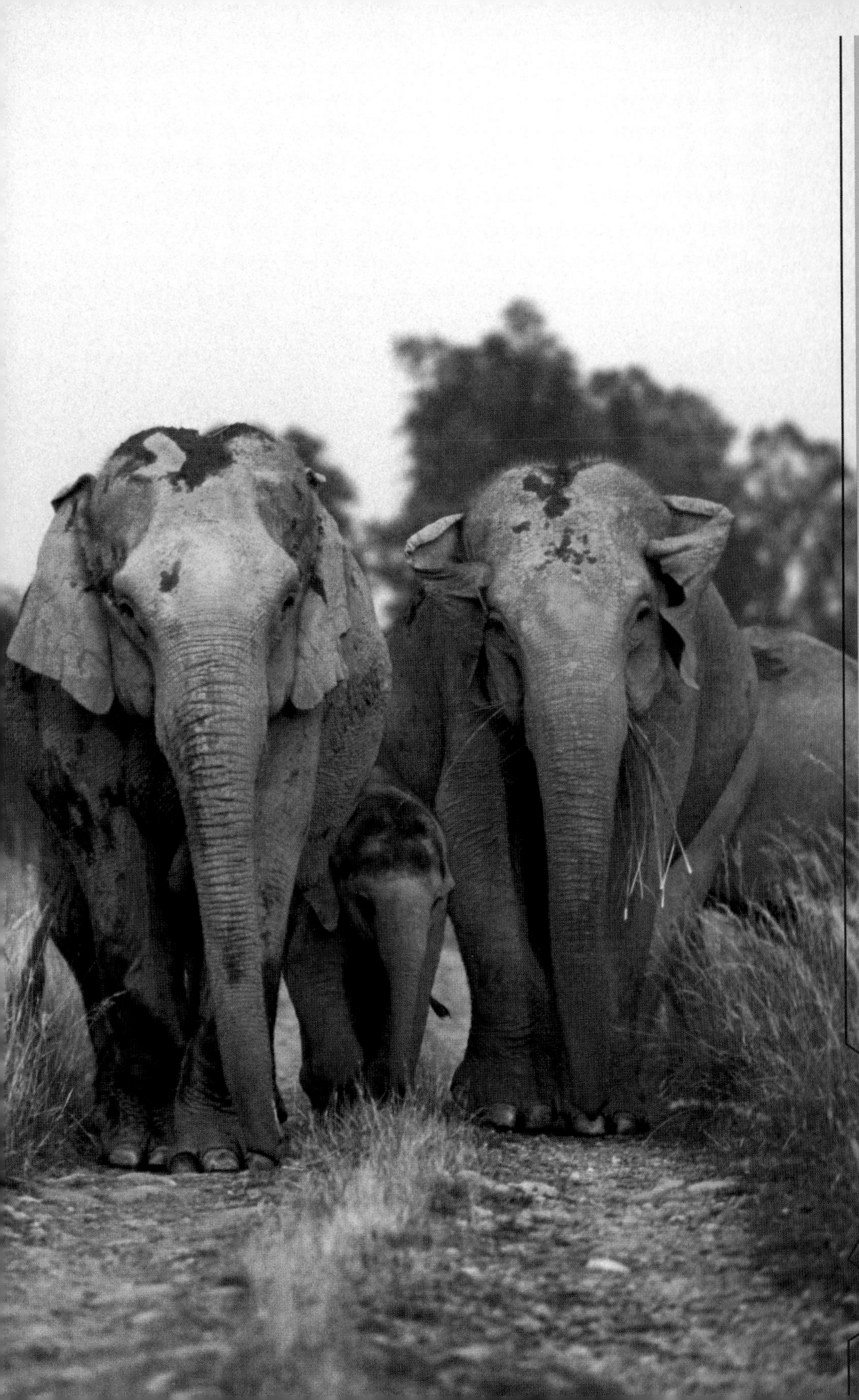

REASON TO CARE # 37

Humans Are Taking Elephant Land

As human populations increase near elephant habitats, land is cleared for new homes. This leaves less space for elephants to forage. Hungry elephants sometimes break into houses and steal food. They also dig up crops to eat.

In west Africa, elephant habitats were reduced by 95 percent in the twentieth century because of human activity. Habitat loss is also a major problem across Asia. Elephant herds are confined to protected areas, such as national parks. Villages and roads block their routes to food and water sources. Conflicts with people and disruptions to the elephant's natural life have threatened its existence.

[Angry farmers kill elephants in retaliation for destroyed crops. In India, angry elephants kill between 200 and 250 people every year.]

◀ CONFLICTS WITH PEOPLE ARE A THREAT TO ELEPHANTS.

Poaching Threatens Elephant Survival

Poachers kill elephants for their ivory tusks. The demand for ivory increased greatly in the last part of the twentieth century because people were using it to make carvings and trinkets. Poachers killed as many elephants as they could in order to sell their ivory. By 1985, Africa was exporting 1,000 tons of ivory per year.

Despite an international ban on most ivory sales, poaching continues. Today, less enforcement of the laws allows more poachers to escape punishment. Many African countries do not have money to stop poaching. Worse, demand for ivory is now increasing in China, Japan, and the United States. As more people desire ivory, the price increases and poachers make more money for the elephants they kill.

[One night, researchers Mark and Delia Owens witnessed gangs of poachers killing elephants in Zambia. Mark and Delia learned that hundreds of elephants were being poached in the area. By educating locals and working with government, they helped put many poachers out of business.]

▶ POACHERS KILL ELEPHANTS FOR THEIR IVORY.

REASON TO CARE # 39

The Ivory Trade
Hurts Elephants

In 1975, the Convention on International Trade in Endangered Species, also known as CITES, was created. All trade of any Asian elephant parts was declared illegal. But as late as 1979, three hundred elephants were still being killed every day in Asia and Africa.

In 1989, the president of Kenya burned ivory valued at $3 million from two thousand poached elephants. He wanted the world to see Kenya's commitment to the ban on the ivory trade. By 1990, CITES declared a ban on trading African elephant ivory. CITES occasionally lifts the total ban on ivory trade and allows countries to sell predetermined amounts of their stored tusks from elephants that died of natural causes.

◀ IT IS IMPORTANT TO STOP THE IVORY TRADE IN ORDER TO SAVE THE ELEPHANTS.

It Is Hard to Tell Legal Ivory from Illegal Ivory

Jewelry, sculptures, buttons, dice, bagpipes, billiard balls, and piano keys are products made of ivory. In the 1970s and 1980s, demand for ivory products rose. Elephants began disappearing by the hundreds every day.

Actions taken by the Convention on International Trade in Endangered Species, also known as CITES, banned the trading of ivory, and the poaching decreased. But there were a lot of ivory tusks sitting unsold in warehouses. The ban prevented them from being sold. CITES eventually agreed to allow African countries to sell tusks from elephants that died naturally as well as ivory taken away from poachers.

Conservationists remain concerned that opening the ivory trade has encouraged poachers. If any ivory is sold, illegal ivory can get mixed in with legal ivory, making it easier and safer for poachers to profit.

[A recent study found that more than twenty-three thousand African elephants were killed between September 2005 and August 2006. The tusks were sold on the black market.]

► CONSERVATIONISTS FEAR THAT ALLOWING ANY LEGAL SALE OF IVORY ENCOURAGES ELEPHANT POACHERS.

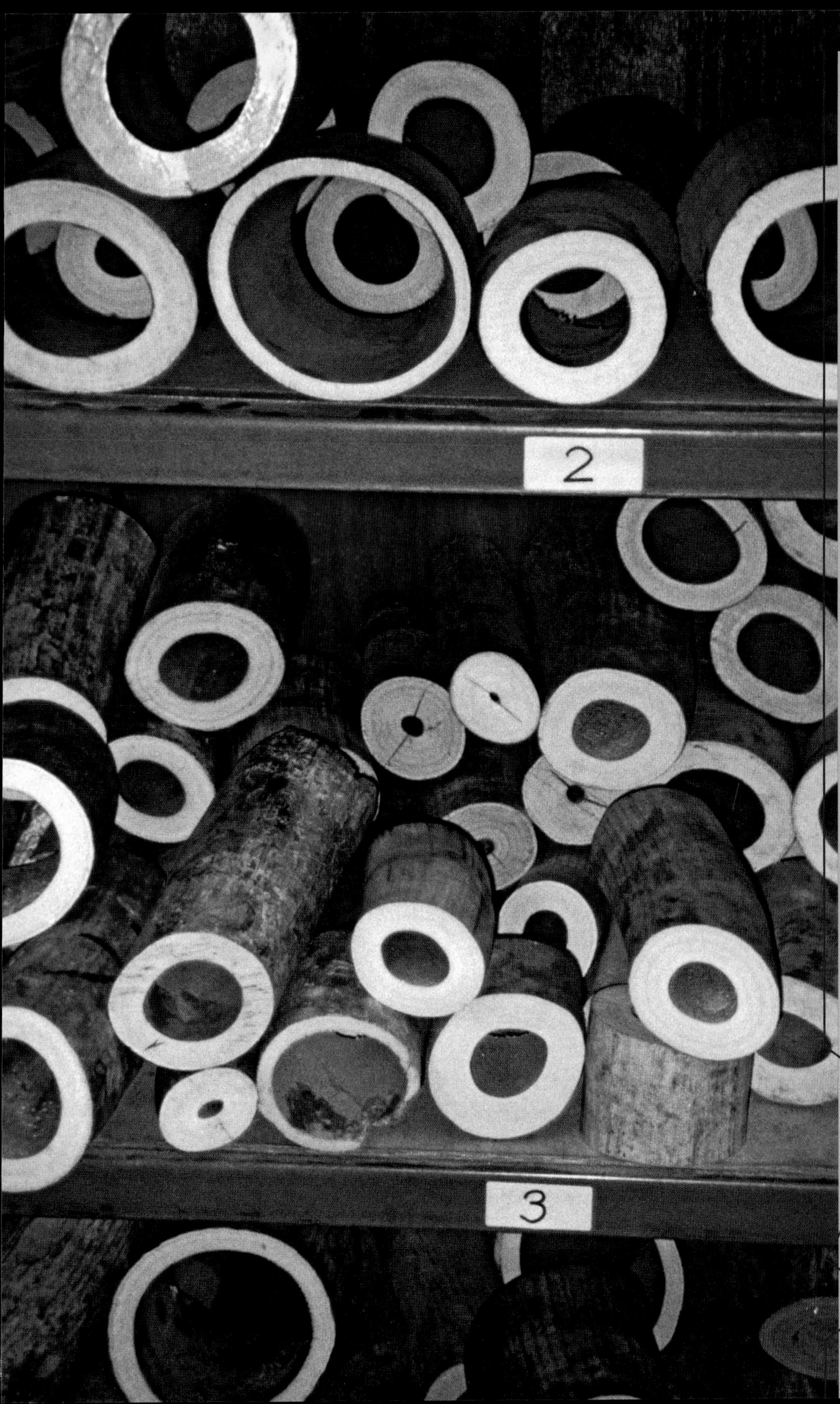
2
3

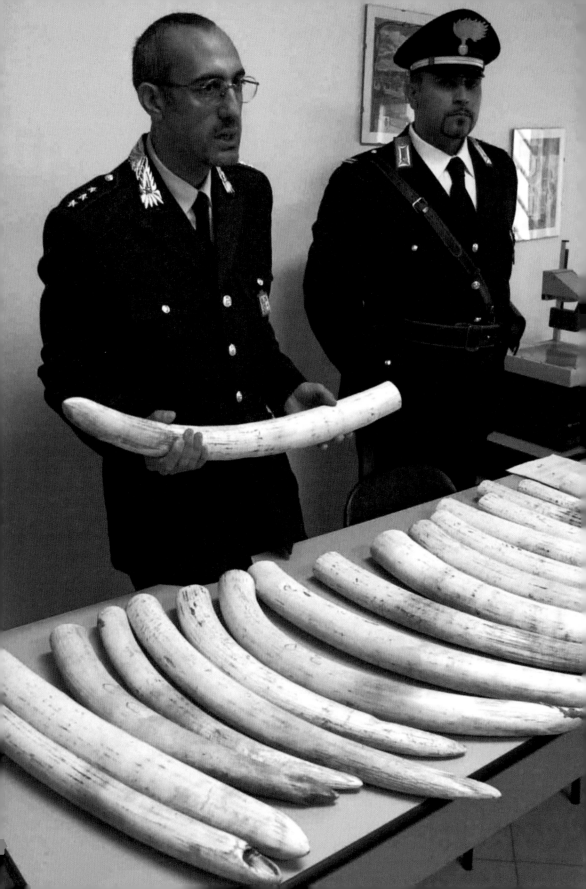

REASON TO CARE # 41

Poaching Can Be Stopped

The dramatic loss of African and Asian elephants in the late twentieth century made one thing very clear: If poaching and habitat loss are not stopped, elephants could become extinct. Conservationists, farmers, and wildlife organizations are protecting habitats. People are working together to control the ivory trade and stop the killing of elephants.

Poachers kill elephants for their ivory, but they also kill elephants for meat and to sell other parts of the bodies. Many countries with elephant populations lack the money to closely monitor poaching. Game scouts watch over elephants and arrest poachers. However, they are often overworked, and sometimes they get killed protecting the elephants. These factors all have an impact on elephants' chances of survival.

◀ GOVERNMENT OFFICIALS WORK TO STOP THE ILLEGAL IVORY TRADE.

REASON TO CARE # 42

Conservation Groups Can Help Elephants

Poaching laws and ivory bans make a big difference in the preservation of elephants, but preserving habitats requires another type of intervention. Save the Elephants Project works with the Association of Private Nature Preserves and National Parks in the Kruger Ecosystem of South Africa. The Kruger National Park in South Africa became a preserve in 1898. It is dedicated to the conservation of African wildlife, including the elephant.

Save the Elephants Project works with members of African communities, involving them in the research and conservation projects. The communities were doubtful about helping elephants at first, because of elephant raids on crops and deaths caused by elephants. After learning that the loss of habitat was the main cause for the elephants' aggressive actions, many communities have taken steps to live peacefully with elephants.

In India, the World Wildlife Fund has created the Asian Rhino and Elephant Action Strategy to create habitats and to empower communities to help save the Asian elephant.

◀ MANY CONSERVATION GROUPS ARE WORKING TO SAVE THE ELEPHANTS.

Protected Reserves Give Elephants Space

Some wild elephants live in protected areas called reserves. One such area is the Amboseli National Park in southern Kenya, where elephants roam in 151 square miles of open space.

Elephants live longer in reserves because their habitat is protected and laws against poaching are enforced. This protected status makes it possible to study several generations of elephant families. Researcher and journalist Cynthia Moss began studying the Amboseli elephants in 1972, witnessing elephant births, deaths, and the dramas of their daily lives. Her work has raised awareness of the elephants' abilities and the difficulties they face.

For the Asian elephant of Thailand, the Western Forest Complex in Southeast Asia is home to 33 percent of its wild elephants. Also in Thailand, the Thung Yai Wildlife Sanctuary hosts conservationists who work with locals as they study how wild elephants live.

▶ LIVING IN PROTECTED RESERVES HELPS ELEPHANT FAMILIES STAY TOGETHER.

ELEPHANT CORRIDOR

Elephant Corridors
Help Elephants Travel

In the past, elephants in India were free to roam. Now their habitats are broken up by highways and farmland. Fragmented habitats have made wildlife corridors a necessity for elephant survival in India.

Corridors are strips of land that connect these fragmented habitats. They make it possible for elephants to move from one area to another. In India, the corridors are critical to preserving elephant populations because conflict with humans over resources is their biggest threat, even more than poaching.

[Two reserves in Karnataka, India, are now linked by a corridor monitored by the Wildlife Trust of India. They will work to ensure this patch of land is safe for elephants.]

◄ CORRIDORS ALLOW ELEPHANTS TO MOVE FROM ONE PROTECTED AREA TO ANOTHER.

Removing Fences
Lets Elephants Roam

Elephants follow ancient migratory routes that stretch for hundreds of miles, crossing borders between African nations. Over time, fences were raised to establish boundaries between nations, preventing elephants from crossing the borders. Villages, fields, roads, and other manmade structures trap elephants in increasingly small ranges in Africa and in Asia. Elephants require wide-open areas to find food and mates.

▼ THIS ELEPHANT IS BEING MOVED FROM KRUGER NATIONAL PARK TO MOZAMBIQUE.

▲ THESE ELEPHANTS ARE PROTECTED IN KRUGER NATIONAL PARK.

The Peace Parks foundation helped make an agreement between some African nations. The nations agreed to take down the fences, allowing elephants to cross borders and reestablish their normal ways of life.

In 2001, a gate between Kruger National Park of South Africa and Mozambique was opened, starting a massive relocation project. Former South African President Nelson Mandela was there to open the gates. Many elephants moved voluntarily, but hundreds were tranquilized and transported by truck to Mozambique.

[Intelligent forest elephants in Africa have learned to associate roads with poachers. One study has shown that forest elephants will not cross roads outside protected areas. The one elephant they found crossing a road rushed across at fourteen times its normal speed.]

Farmers Can Protect Their Crops from Elephants

Farmers are angry. Once again, herds of elephants thunder through crops, trampling and eating what lies in their path. The situation has caused Asian and African farmers to lose millions of dollars in crops each year, and farmers and elephants have died in the struggle.

Elephants and humans both require land, food, and water to survive. In addition to traditional conservation methods, scientists and farmers are coming up with some clever ideas. In Zimbabwe, farmers use a type of chili pepper smoke bomb. They plant chili peppers and then burn a few of them. The chili-scented smoke keeps elephants away from crops, and farmers sell the rest of the chilies at market. In Asia, some fruit growers have switched to dairy farming rather than trying to stop the elephants.

[Scientist Raman Sukumar moved to a forest hut where he could watch elephants night and day. He found that elephants prefer cereal crops such as rice or wheat to natural grasses. These crops taste better and have more of the minerals and protein elephants need.]

▶ THIS ELEPHANT FEEDS IN A SUGAR CANE FIELD. FARMERS ARE LEARNING NEW METHODS TO KEEP ELEPHANTS AWAY.

REASON TO CARE # 47
Collars Teach Scientists About Elephant Life

Researchers fired a tranquilizer dart at Goya, the 6,000-pound (2,700-kilogram) matriarch living with her herd near Sambura, Kenya. As she fell to the ground, it was clear the tranquilizer had taken effect. Scientists ran to her side to quickly collect blood, hair, and skin samples and fit her with a radio collar. She was back on her feet in ten minutes, unharmed and with her family.

Elephant collars are equipped with electronics, such as Global Positioning Systems (GPS), which track elephant locations and levels of activity by satellite. This data helps scientists learn more about elephant needs.

Scientists also use GPS collars on elephants because they need to know the paths the elephants have taken. This helps the scientists find the areas where elephants have trampled huts and crops.

◄ SCIENTISTS FIT AN ELEPHANT WITH A TRACKING COLLAR.

Elephant Orphans Can Be Saved

When poachers kill a female elephant, a baby elephant often loses a mother. If several females in a herd are killed, and if no other herd is nearby, the very young elephant will not survive on its own. It depends on its mother's milk for the first two years of its life.

▼ LUCKY ORPHANED ELEPHANTS ARE RAISED IN SANCTUARIES.

▲ BABY ELEPHANTS MUST DRINK MILK FOR THEIR FIRST
TWO YEARS OF LIFE.

Sometimes, humans are able to rescue young elephants that have lost their herds. The Nairobi Elephant Nursery cares for these orphaned calves. They are kept safe. Later, they are able to bond with other elephants.

[In 1977, Daphne Sheldrick created the Nairobi Elephant Nursery in Nairobi National Park. By 2005, she had hand-raised sixty-seven orphaned elephants. She developed a deep understanding and respect for elephants during the years she worked with them.]

Zoo Elephants
Help Scientists Learn

A study by the Royal Society for the Prevention of Cruelty to Animals found that elephants in European zoos were frequently unhealthy and lived shorter lives than they would in the wild.

However, scientists argue that elephants in captivity are important to conservation. Captive elephants are easier for scientists to study. The data they can collect from these studies can help elephants in the wild.

▼ ZOO TRAINERS WORK HARD TO KEEP THEIR ELEPHANTS HAPPY AND HEALTHY.

▲ KIDS AND GROWN-UPS VISIT ZOOS TO LEARN MORE ABOUT ELEPHANTS.

Many zoos work hard to keep elephants happy and comfortable. For example, at the San Diego Zoo in California, elephants receive regular rubdowns with mineral oil to protect their sensitive skin. Elephants need these special treatments, which would normally be provided by nature in their habitat.

Also, by educating visitors about the dangers to elephants, people who visit zoos leave with a better understanding that elephants need protection.

You Can Help Save Elephants

Fun and Rewarding Ways to Help Save Elephants

- Read books, magazines, and newspaper articles about elephants.
- Visit zoos where there are elephants so you can see them up close.
- Do not buy ivory.
- Ask your local zoo if they need volunteers.
- Help your class plan a fund-raiser to support an organization that protects elephants.
- Talk to your school principal or teacher about fostering an African baby elephant.
- Keep informed. Read updates on elephant populations on the World Wildlife Fund and Nature Conservancy Web sites.
- Recycle and use less energy. Cutting back may help reduce climate change, which affects elephant habitat.
- Write an article for your school newspaper about elephants.

► YOU CAN HELP SAVE THE ELEPHANT!

GLOSSARY

captivity—Being in a zoo instead of the wild.

conservation—The protection of nature and animals.

endangered—At risk of becoming extinct.

environment—The natural world; the area in which a
person or animal lives.

extinct—Died out completely.

forage—To look for food.

habitat—The place in which an animal lives; the
features of that place including plants, landforms,
and weather.

herbivore—An animal that eats only plants.

Hindu—A person who practices Hinduism, a religion
that began in India.

incisor—A tooth at the front of the mouth that is used
for cutting.

infrasound—Very low sounds, below human ability to
hear.

ivory—The material of an elephant's tusks.

mahout—A person who trains elephants.

malnutrition—Not having enough food or eating the
wrong kinds of food.

mammal—A warm-blooded animal with hair; female mammals nurse their young.

matriarch—A mother and leader.

membrane—A thin layer of tissue or skin.

molar—A tooth located in the back of the mouth used for grinding food.

order—A category of similar families, or groups, of animals.

poach—To illegally kill or steal protected wild animals.

population—The total number of a group of animals.

prehistoric—From a time before written history.

range—The entire area in which a species lives; the territory of an individual animal or group of animals.

reserve—A protected area for animals to live.

savanna—A grassland with scattered trees and shrubs.

species—A specific group of animals with shared physical characteristics and genes; members within a species can breed with each other to produce offspring.

wallow—To roll around in mud or water.

FURTHER READING

Books

Bloom, Steve. *Elephant*. San Francisco, CA: Chronicle Books, 2006.

Brandt, Nick. *On This Earth: Photographs From East Africa*. San Francisco, CA: Chronicle Books, 2005.

Joubert, Derreck, and Beverly Joubert. *Face to Face With Elephants*. Washington, DC: National Geographic Children's Books, 2008.

Poole, Joyce. *Elephants*. Stillwater, MN: Voyageur Press, 1997.

Internet Addresses

Animal Planet—Elephant Rescue
<http://animal.discovery.com/convergence/safari/
elephant/elephant.html>

The David Sheldrick Wildlife Trust
<http://www.sheldrickwildlifetrust.org/index.asp>

World Wildlife Fund—Elephants
<http://www.worldwildlife.org/species/finder/elephants/
item560.html>

INDEX